YOUR KNOWLEDGE HAS VALUE

Dang Xuan Tho

Perceptron Problem in Neural Network

GRIN Publishing

Bibliographic information published by the German National Library:

The German National Library lists this publication in the National Bibliography; detailed bibliographic data are available on the Internet at http://dnb.dnb.de .

Imprint:

Copyright © 2010 GRIN Verlag GmbH
Print and binding: Books on Demand GmbH, Norderstedt Germany
ISBN: 978-3-640-64895-5

This book at GRIN:

http://www.grin.com/en/e-book/153037/perceptron-problem-in-neural-network

GRIN - Your knowledge has value

Since its foundation in 1998, GRIN has specialized in publishing academic texts by students, college teachers and other academics as e-book and printed book. The website www.grin.com is an ideal platform for presenting term papers, final papers, scientific essays, dissertations and specialist books.

Visit us on the internet:

http://www.grin.com/

http://www.facebook.com/grincom

http://www.twitter.com/grin_com

NEURAL NETWORK

Perceptron

Perceptron Problem

Consider a perceptron shown in Fig 9.1. The input data $x = [x_1, x_2]^T$

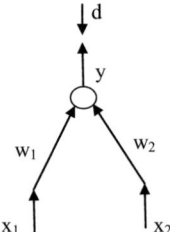

Figure 9.1: Perceptron with two-dimensional input data.

and the output y are related by

$$v = w_1 x_1 + w_2 x_2 = w^T x \tag{9.1}$$

$$y = \psi(v) = \begin{cases} 1, v \geq 0 \\ 0, v < 0 \end{cases} \tag{9.2}$$

The input data $x \in C_1$ and $x \in C_1$ are distributed during 60 ~ 120 degrees and 225 ~340 degrees as shown in Fig 9.2.

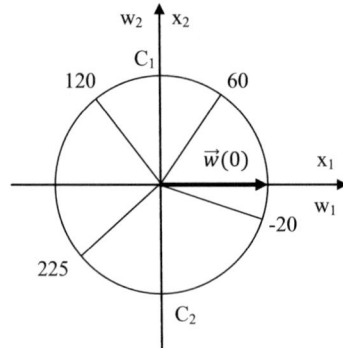

Figure 9.2: Input data distribution. Input data $x \in C_1$ and $x \in C_1$ are distributed during 60 ~ 120 degrees and 225 ~340 degrees. Initial connection weight w(0) locates at 0 degrees.

The data x is randomly sample in both classes, and applied to the perceptron. The connection weights are updated following

$$d(n) = \begin{cases} 1, x \in C_1 \\ 0, x \in C_2 \end{cases} \tag{9.3}$$

$$e(n) = d(n) - y(n) \tag{9.4}$$

$$w(0) = [1,0]^T \tag{9.5}$$

$$w(n+1) = w(n) + \eta e(n)x(n) \tag{9.6}$$

$$\|x(n)\| = 1 \tag{9.7}$$

$$w(n+1) = \frac{w(n+1)}{\|w(n+1)\|} \tag{9.8}$$

The inner product of w and x and an angle θ, shown in Fig 9.3 between them are related by

$$\cos\theta = \frac{w^T x}{\|w\|\|x\|} \tag{9.9}$$

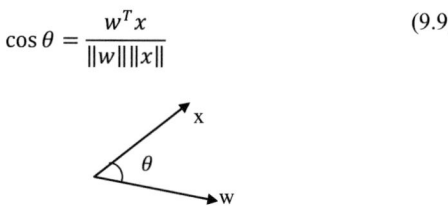

Figure 9.3: Relation between inner product of two vectors and angle between them

Please show the regions, where the final weight vector w can locate, in the following two cases. The regions should be indicated by an angle.

a. η is large.
b. η is very small.

And answer some question

1. Obtain the region, where optimum connection weight can locate.
2. Direction of adjustment.

The input potential v can be expressed by

$$v = w^T x = \frac{w^T x}{\|w\|\|x\|}, \|w\| = \|x\| = 1 \tag{9.10}$$

Substituting Eq. (9.9) in Eq. (9.10), we get [1]

$$v = \cos(\theta) \tag{9.11}$$

Therefore, v $\geq$ 0 and v < 0 are the same as $|\theta| \leq \frac{\pi}{2}$ and $|\theta| > \frac{\pi}{2}$, respectively.

The initial weight vector is set to be w(0) = [1,0], as shown in Fig.9.2. Its angle is 135 degrees [1].

When the input data of C_2 is distributed during **270 ~ 340 degrees**, applied to the perceptron, we get

$$|\theta| < \frac{\pi}{2} \tag{9.12}$$

$$\cos(\theta) > 0 \tag{9.13}$$

$$d(n) = 0, x \in C_2 \tag{9.14}$$

Substituting Eq. (9.13) in Eq. (9.11) we get
$$v \geq 0 \tag{9.15}$$
Substituting Eq. (9.15) in Eq. (9.2) we get
$$y = 1 \tag{9.16}$$
Substituting Eq. (9.14) and (9.16) in Eq. (9.4) we get
$$e(n) = -1 \tag{9.17}$$
$$w(n+1) = w(n) - \eta x(n) \tag{9.18}$$

So, if the input data of C_2 is distributed during 270 ~ 340 degrees, the weight vector is rotated counterclockwise [2, 3], as shown in Fig.9.4

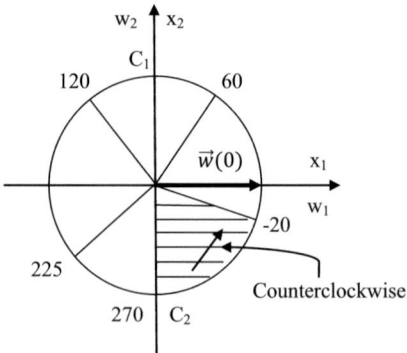

Figure 9.4: When the input data of C_2 is distributed during 270 ~ 340 degrees, applied to the perceptron, the weight vector is rotated counterclockwise.

When the input data of C_2 is distributed during **225 ~ 270 degrees**, applied to the perceptron, we get

$$|\theta| > \frac{\pi}{2} \qquad (9.19)$$
$$\cos(\theta) < 0 \qquad (9.20)$$
$$d(n) = 0, x \in C_2 \qquad (9.21)$$

Substituting Eq. (9.20) in Eq. (9.11) we get

$$v < 0 \qquad (9.22)$$

Substituting Eq. (9.22) in Eq. (9.2) we get

$$y = 0 \qquad (9.23)$$

Substituting Eq. (9.21) and (9.23) in Eq. (9.4) we get

$$e(n) = 0 \qquad (9.24)$$
$$w(n+1) = w(n) \qquad (9.25)$$

So, if the input data of C_2 is distributed during 225 ~ 270 degrees, the weight vector is no adjustment, as shown in Fig.9.5

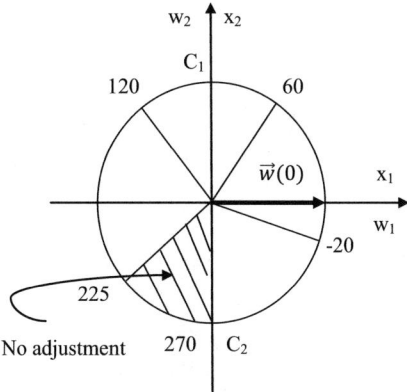

Figure 9.5: When the input data of C_2 is distributed during 225 ~ 270 degrees, applied to the perceptron, the weight vector is no adjustment.

In the same way, when the input data of C_2 is distributed during **60 ~ 90 degrees**, applied to the perceptron, we get

$$|\theta| < \frac{\pi}{2} \qquad (9.26)$$

$$\cos(\theta) > 0 \qquad (9.27)$$

$$d(n) = 1, x \in C_1 \qquad (9.28)$$

Substituting Eq. (9.27) in Eq. (9.11) we get

$$v > 0 \qquad (9.29)$$

Substituting Eq. (9.29) in Eq. (9.2) we get

$$y = 1 \qquad (9.30)$$

Substituting Eq. (9.28) and (9.30) in Eq. (9.4) we get

$$e(n) = 0 \qquad (9.31)$$

$$w(n+1) = w(n) \qquad (9.32)$$

So, if the input data of C_1 is distributed during 60 ~ 90 degrees, the weight vector is no adjustment, as shown in Fig.9.6

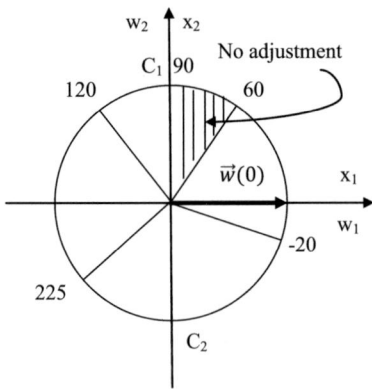

Figure 9.6: When the input data of C_1 is distributed during 60 ~ 90 degrees, applied to the perceptron, the weight vector is no adjustment.

On the other hand, when the input data of C_1 is distributed during **90 ~ 120 degrees**, applied to the perceptron, we get

$$|\theta| > \frac{\pi}{2} \tag{9.33}$$

$$\cos(\theta) < 0 \tag{9.34}$$

$$d(n) = 1, x \in C_1 \tag{9.35}$$

Substituting Eq. (9.34) in Eq. (9.11) we get

$$v < 0 \tag{9.36}$$

Substituting Eq. (9.36) in Eq. (9.2) we get

$$y = 0 \tag{9.37}$$

Substituting Eq. (9.35) and (9.37) in Eq. (9.4) we get

$$e(n) = 1 \tag{9.38}$$

$$w(n+1) = w(n) + \eta x(n) \tag{9.39}$$

So, if the input data of C_1 is distributed during 60 ~ 90 degrees, the weight vector is rotated clockwise, as shown in Fig.9.7

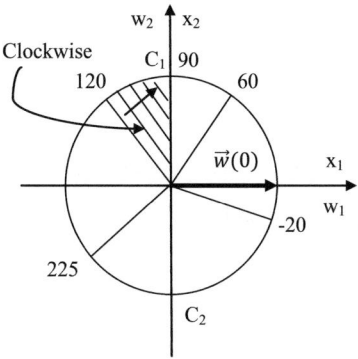

Figure 9.7: When the input data of C_1 is distributed during 90 ~ 120 degrees, applied to the perceptron, the weight vector is rotated clockwise.

The region, in which the input data are distributed, and the weight vector is adjusted counterclockwise is larger than the other region. Therefore, the weight vector is updated counterclockwise. The final destination becomes $w(\infty) = [\cos(70), \sin(70)]^T$, whose angle is 70 degrees. [1] Because the output y = 1 for all data in C_1 and y = 0 for all data in C_2, no adjustment is required, as shown in Fig.9.8.

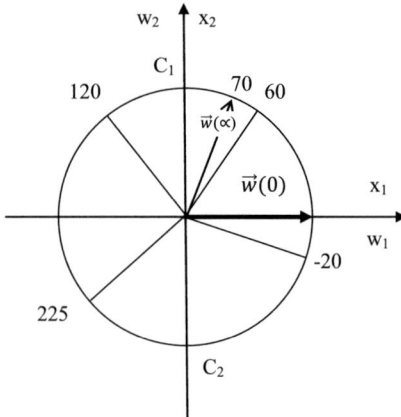

Figure 9.7: When final destination becomes $w(\infty) = [\cos(70), \sin(70)]^T$, whose angle is 70 degrees. The output y = 1 for all data in C_1 and y = 0 for all data in C_2, no adjustment is required.

The region, where optimum connection weight can locate have to satisfy

$$\begin{cases} x(n) \in C_1, v = w^T(n)x(n) \geq 0 & \text{(9.40a)} \\ x(n) \in C_2, v = w^T(n)x(n) < 0 & \text{(9.40b)} \end{cases}$$

That is the reason, the weight vector cannot locate over 150 degrees to satisfy Eq. (9.40a).

On the other hand, if the weight vector move over 150 degrees, and input data of C_1 distributed during 60 ~ 120 degrees, so the angle $\theta > 90$ degrees.

$$\cos(\theta) < 0 \qquad (9.41)$$

Substituting Eq. (9.41) in Eq. (9.11) we get

$$v < 0 \qquad (9.42)$$

Eq. (9.42) made the condition Eq. (9.40a) do not satisfy, as shown in the Fig. 9.8

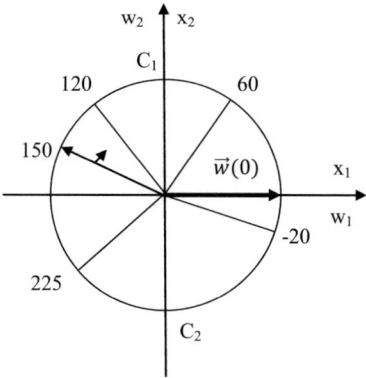

Figure 9.8: The weight vector can not locate over 150 degrees to satisfy Eq. (9.40a).

In the same way, the weight vector can not locate over 135 degrees to satisfy Eq. (9.40b), as shown in the Fig.9.9.

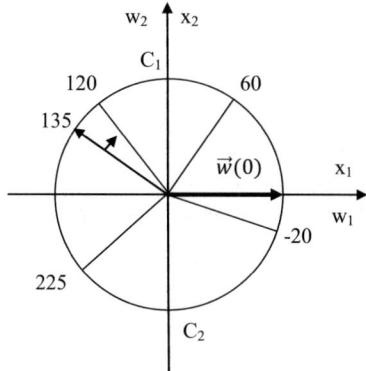

Figure 9.9: The weight vector can not locate over 135 degrees to satisfy Eq. (9.40b).

Therefore, the final region, where optimum connection weight vector can locate distribute during 70 ~ 135 degrees, as shown in Fig. 9.10.

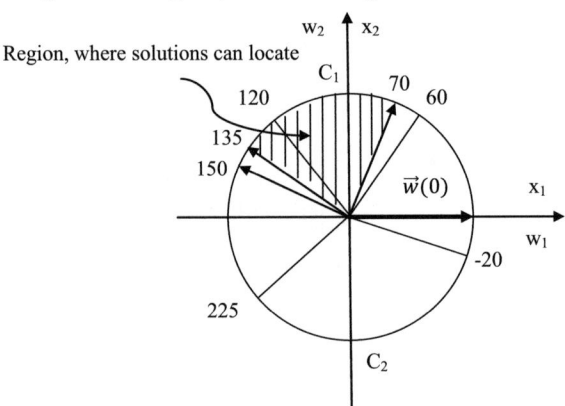

Figure 9.10: the final region, where optimum connection weight vector can locate distribute during 70 ~ 135 degrees.

Following the Eq. (9.18), the weight vector is rotated counterclockwise, and the Eq. (9.39), the weight vector is rotated clockwise.

$$w(n+1) = w(n) - \eta x(n) \qquad (9.18)$$

$$w(n+1) = w(n) + \eta x(n) \qquad (9.39)$$

In the first case, substituting η is large in Eq. (9.18) and Eq. (9.39), the value of $w(n+1)$ change very much. It can move to the $w(\infty)$, whose angle is 70 degrees, very quick. However, it does not stop exactly at the angle 70 degrees.

On the other hand, in the second case, substituting η is very small in Eq. (9.18) and Eq. (9.39), the value of $w(n+1)$ change very little. It can move to the $w(\infty)$, whose angle is 70 degrees, very slowly. However, it may stop at the angle 70 degrees.

So, we have to define the right the value of η to change $w(n+1)$ much and quick stop at the final destination.

References

[1] Kenji Nakayama, "Adaptive System Theory – Neural Network –", 2010, Kanazawa.

[2] James A. Anderson, "An introduction to neural network", 1995, ISBN 0262011441, Cambridge, Mass, MIT Press.

[3] Bernard Widrow, "30 years of adaptive Neural Network: Perceptron, Madaline, and Backpropagation", Vol. 78, No. 9 September 1990.